FISHING
THE LOCAL
WATERS

(Gulf Shores to Panama City)

Third Edition

Also available from Maximum Press...

Fishing The Local Waters: (West Palm Beach to Miami), Hoskins

Distributed by
JH Sales
3242 West Avenue
Gulf Breeze, FL 32561

(904) 932-2583

FISHING
THE LOCAL
WATERS

(Gulf Shores to Panama City)

Third Edition

Jim Hoskins
Illustrated by Ed Ilano

Maximum Press
a division of Maximum Ventures Corporation
605 Silverthorn Road
Gulf Breeze, Florida 32561

Printed in the United States of America

10 9 8

To Monica ... my best fishing buddy,
To Nikolas ... my future fishing buddy,
and
To my parents ... who first taught me to fish

Acknowledgments

Many people assisted with the development of this book. Some provided valuable input while others reviewed the contents for accuracy and completeness. To those who helped, I thank you. I would especially like to thank Joyce Allyn, Katie Bell, Sherry Broom, Don Guest, Edward Ilano, Sim Levay, Steve McWilliams, and Maribel Rayos.

Disclaimer

Fishing laws are subject to change without notice. Local authorities should always be consulted by the reader to insure a complete understanding of the current laws.

While some local boating safety information is provided in this book, it is not intended to replace safe boating publications or classes provided by the U. S. Coast Guard. This book assumes that the reader understands basic boating safety. All navigational information contained in this book is for reference purposes only. Use only current U. S. Coast Guard charts and "Local Notice To Mariners" publications for navigation. Some LORAN coordinates contained in this book have not been verified.

Finally, sea conditions and currents can turn normally safe swimming and boating areas into treacherous waters. Swimming is recommended only in lifeguard protected areas.

As a result of the foregoing, the author assumes no liability whatsoever for the continued accuracy of the information contained herein and disclaims any and all warranties, expressed or implied, as to the accuracy of said information.

Contents

Introduction

What This Book Is

Nothing is more frustrating than arriving in a new city, fishing rod in hand, and not knowing the details about fishing in the area. Even where the fishing is excellent, such as in the waters around the Miracle Strip (i.e., Gulf Shores, Pensacola, Ft. Walton, Destin, and Panama City), an experienced fisherman can come away empty handed if not equipped with local fishing information. You need the answers to many questions such as, "Where, exactly, are the best fishing spots?", "What kind of bait should I use?", and "What types of rigs and techniques are most effective on the local fish?" Fishing the Miracle Strip is very different from fishing in South Florida or fishing inland lakes or fishing the Eastern Seaboard. In each of these cases, the kinds of fish are different, as are the types of baits, rigs, and techniques that are most effective.

That's just where this book comes in. It is a complete guide to saltwater fishing in the fertile waters around the Miracle Strip. It provides detailed information on some proven fishing spots, baits, and techniques. Fishing from shore is covered as well as fishing from a boat. The types of fish you are likely to catch are discussed and fish identification charts are provided to help you sort out the good eating fish from the rest. Also included is a collection of local seafood recipes that are favorites in the area.

Whether you just want to spend a lazy afternoon fishing from shore or go on a full-scale boating excursion into the Gulf of Mexico, this book will equip you with the knowledge necessary to waste less time and catch more fish.

What This Book Is Not

Many fishing books try to be all things to all people. They start by explaining fly casting in mountain streams and finish by covering marlin fishing in Mexico. While these books are interesting, they do not provide information specific to a local area. They therefore leave many unanswered questions, such as, "Exactly where do I go?" and "Which rigs, baits, and techniques should I use when I get there?"

This book is not a general overview of fishing. It is specific to saltwater fishing locations, rigs, baits, and techniques proven to be productive in Northwest Florida and adjacent waters (a more than broad enough subject for a single book). This book will not teach you how to catch salmon off Alaska, nor will it get you ready for fishing the lakes in Canada. It will, instead, teach you -- step by step -- how to catch fish in the local waters around the Miracle Strip.

How to Use This Book

Chapter 1 discusses the tackle, rigs, baits, and techniques used to fish the local inland waters. Bottom fishing, dealing with live shrimp, and lure fishing are discussed. Popular inland fishing locations are listed and described, as are the types of fish you are likely to catch.

Chapter 2 discusses the tackle, rigs, baits, and techniques used to fish the Gulf waters from the beaches, jetties, or piers. Techniques for catching live bait are explained, as are several effective fishing methods. Popular Gulf fishing spots are listed and described.

Chapter 3 discusses the tackle, rigs, baits, and techniques used to fish the Gulf waters from a boat. The types of fish caught by offshore Gulf fishermen are discussed. Trolling, bottom fishing, drift fishing, and cast fishing are covered. LORAN C Lines of Position are given for many Gulf fishing spots accessible by boat. Some local boating safety information is also provided.

Chapter 4 offers some recipes for preparing fish that are local favorites. These recipes were collected from many different cooks along the Miracle Strip.

Appendix A, "Fish Identification Charts," provides sketches of many fish commonly caught in the local waters. These can help you identify the fish you catch.

Appendix B, "Area Maps," contains the local maps that pinpoint the fishing spots discussed in this book.

"The Fisherman's Directory" at the back of this book is an alphabetical listing of many local merchants that cater to fishermen.

To help you better understand the topics covered in this book, key terms and phrases are defined and given in **boldface** when they are first introduced. These key terms are also listed in the index at the back of this book. If while reading you forget the definition of a key term or phrase defined elsewhere, the index will quickly point you to the page(s) where the term is discussed.

Environmentally Friendly Fishing

Fishing can be both relaxing and exciting. And nothing tastes better than freshly caught and well-prepared fish. While you are fishing, please help preserve the fishery and environment for those who follow both tomorrow and in years to come. We do not inherit the fishery from our parents; we borrow it from our children.

Here are some tips to help preserve the marine fishery and the environment:

* **Please throw back any fish you don't want to eat or mount.** Bring your camera and take pictures of the fish before you throw them back; photos make great trophies. Handle the fish gently and with wet hands.

* **Please follow the bag limit laws.** State and federal laws have been passed to prevent over-fishing of various species. It is important to the long-term vitality of our waters that these laws be obeyed. The Florida Marine Patrol and the Alabama Marine Police actively enforce these laws, many of which carry heavy fines for violations.

* Please report any violations of marine fishery laws. You can do this by calling the Resource Alert line: (800) DIAL-FMP.

* Please pick up any floating garbage. You can make a difference and perhaps save the lives of marine creatures by simply picking up any floating garbage you may come across. Sea birds, turtles, and fish can eat or become entangled in the garbage. Besides, who wants to see garbage floating around? Of course, don't throw any garbage (including cigarette butts) into the water.

* Please avoid dripping gas or oil in the water while refueling. If you do spill gas or oil, you can spray a solution of soap and water from a spray bottle onto the spill to help break it up.

Chapter

| 1 |

Fishing the Inland Waters

The **inland waters** around the Miracle Strip offer convenient, inexpensive fishing that can be both relaxing and rewarding. For the purposes of this book, inland waters include the intracoastal waterways and bays between the Miracle Strip islands and the mainland (See Appendix B, "Area Maps.") For the boater, the inland waters are protected from winds, making for smoother waters and added safety compared with the Gulf of Mexico. For those without a boat, the many piers and shore locations listed in this chapter provide good fishing access to these waters. This chapter will survey some commonly caught fish and proven locations, baits, rigs, and techniques for fishing the inland waters.

What You Are Likely to Catch

While fishing the inland waters, you can catch fish that are good to eat. Some of the most common catches are listed in Figure 1-1.

Baits/Rigs/Techniques

Almost any type of fishing rod and reel can be used to fish the inland waters with any of the techniques described in this chapter. The weight of the tackle used (i.e., rod stiffness, line strength, reel size, etc.) is a

Type	Eating Quality	Active Periods	Typical Size (lbs.)
White Trout	good	March-August	1 to 6
Speckled Trout	good	Sept. - April	2 to 10
Croaker	fair	All year	1 to 6
Spanish Mackerel	excellent	March - May	2 to 15
Redfish	excellent	Sept. - Dec.	5 to 40
Sheepshead	good	Sept. - April	2 to 10
Flounder	good	All year	2 to 10

Figure1-1: Fish commonly caught in the inland waters. See Appendix A, "Fish Identification Charts," for drawings of these fish.

matter of personal choice. Light-weight tackle (e.g., light-action rod, closed-face reel, 10 lb. test line) as shown in Figure 1-2 will test the fisherman's skill allowing even the smaller fish to put up an interesting fight.

Heavier weight tackle (e.g., medium-action rod, medium open-face reel, 20 lb. test line) as shown in Figure 1-3 will allow you to land a fish more quickly and will also allow easier handling of the bigger fish should you be particularly lucky. You may even want to consider heavier line (e.g., 25 lb. test) if you will be fishing from the bridges (described later in this section) since it will often be necessary to lift the full weight of the fish from the surface up to bridge level.

After you have a rod and reel picked out, you must decide how you would like to fish. Some productive methods for fishing the local inland

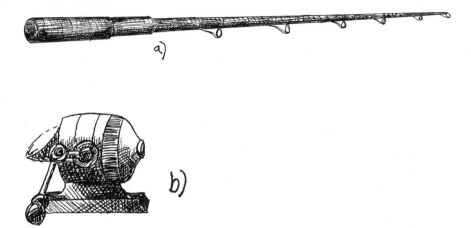

Figure1-2: Light tackle suitable for inland water fishing.
(a) closed-face reel. (b) Casting rod.

waters include:

* Bottom fishing
* Fishing with live shrimp
* Fishing with lures
* Specializing for speckled trout

Bottom Fishing

The most common form of fishing the local inland waters is **bottom fishing**. The baits most commonly used include **shrimp, squid,** or **cut mullet** (a local fish). Redfish, white trout, croaker, and sheepshead are often caught with this technique. Figure 1-4 shows a bottom fishing rig that can be used with any of these bait types. This rig consists of a **double-drop** leader, a #4 **treble hook,** and a two-ounce **pyramid weight.** The double-drop leader allows you to offer two baits to the fish with every cast. Since fish are good at stealing the bait off the hooks, having two baits means they will have to work twice as hard to leave you empty-handed.

There are several variations on the double-drop leader available in any tackle shop, but all will produce about the same results. Most like simple leaders made of heavy **monofilament** line (a translucent plastic strand) rather than steel since they are less visible to the fish. The treble hooks each provide three points to hold the bait more securely and to more easily hook fish. A #4 hook is large enough for most fish you are likely to encounter and small enough to be bite size. The hooks are attached to the leader through clips that are much like safety pins.

The pyramid weight, named after its shape, is designed to stick into soft bottoms, like those in local waters; thus providing more holding power against currents. The pyramid weight is also attached to a safety-pin-type clip on the very

Figure 1-3: Medium-weight tackle suitable for inland water fishing.

bottom of the leader. A two-ounce weight will suit most situations, providing a good casting weight while not overloading your rod. If you find that your line is drifting to freely with the current, try going to a three- or four-ounce pyramid weight.

A **swivel** is usually provided at the top of the leader and is used as a place to tie on the fishing line and also to prevent line twisting by rotating as necessary. The knot used to tie the leader onto your fishing line is very important. An improper knot can excessively weaken the line causing the line to break under the load of a fish. The **fisherman's knot** is easy to tie and can be used for tying any type of rig onto your fishing line no matter where or how you are fishing. Figure 1-5 shows how this knot is tied.

After the leader is tied to the line, you are ready to bait your hooks. As mentioned earlier, the most commonly used baits include shrimp, squid, and cut mullet. Shrimp often gets better results than the other two, but it is more expensive and harder to keep on your hook. Squid and cut mullet are tougher and can sometimes get fish biting when shrimp are not producing strikes. Shrimp will stay on the hook better if they are fresh (i.e., never been frozen). Many bait shops in the area sell fresh shrimp. Alternatively, frozen shrimp can be thawed under running tap water and used. In either case, remove the shrimp head and peel the shell off the tail. Then wrap the shrimp tail around the treble hook so that each of the three prongs pierces the shrimp tail. Make sure all barbs of the hook are visible. This makes it easier to hook a fish.

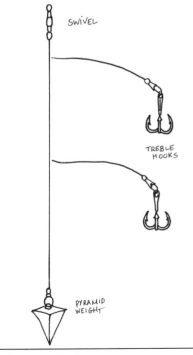

Figure 1-4: Double-drop bottom fishing rig.

Squid is much tougher than shrimp and will therefore stay on a hook better. Squid is almost always sold frozen and can be thawed under running water if necessary. With a bait knife, cut the squid into strips about four inches long. Wrap the squid around the treble hook, again piercing each of the three prongs of

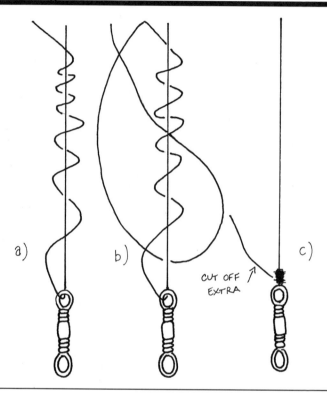

CUT OFF
EXTRA

Figure 1-5: Tying the fisherman's knot. (a) First feed the line through the swivel part of the leader. Then wrap the loose end of the line around itself five to seven times. (b) Feed the end of the line through the loop created near the swivel and then back through the second loop just created. (c) Then gently pull on the line and the knot will draw down to the swivel. Cut off any excess line to complete the knot.

the treble hook through the meat at least once. Don't leave any long trails of squid hanging away from the hooks as they allow the fish to avoid the hook and still get a bite. Since squid is so tough, it is even more important than usual to make sure the barbs of each prong are visible after baiting the hook.

Mullet is an inexpensive fish that can be cut up for bait. To use Mullet, cut strips from the body of the fish about one-half-inch wide and four inches long. Wrap the strip around the treble hook, piercing the flesh with each barb at least once. As always, make sure the barbs are visible after baiting the hook.

When your hooks are baited, cast the line into the water and allow it to sink completely to the bottom. Slack will develop in the line when the weight hits the bottom. Quickly retrieve any slack in the line and make it just taut being careful not to slide the weight along the bottom. Usually you will not have to wait long for bites. When you feel either steady tugging or one pronounced tug, snatch the rod tip toward the sky with a strong upward motion and wind the reel. When bringing in the fish, take care to keep the slack out of the line or you could lose the fish. As always, be sure to release any fish you don't want to eat.

Fishing with Live Shrimp

Usually, live shrimp will provide better results than dead bait because of the movements made by the shrimp as well as its more natural smell and taste. Speckled trout are especially fond of live shrimp. You can buy live shrimp by the dozen at local bait stores, and then it's your job to keep them from turning into dead shrimp. A styrofoam ice chest or a bait bucket filled with saltwater can be used to keep the shrimp alive. In either case, try to keep the shrimp in the shade to prevent the water from getting too hot, which will quickly kill them. Periodically scoop up some fresh saltwater with another container and pour it into the container of live shrimp. This will help keep them alive. **Oxygen tablets** or an **air pump** can also be used to extend the life of the shrimp.

The bottom fishing rig and technique described in the last section can be used with live shrimp except, of course, don't remove the head and shell of the live shrimp. When fish are actively biting, simply wrap the live shrimp around the treble hook as you do with dead shrimp piercing the body with each of the three prongs. Even though this will limit the mobility of the live shrimp, the limited motion as well as the fresh smell and taste makes live shrimp more appetizing to the fish.

In situations where the fish are not actively biting, try using a **shrimp harness** (shown in Figure 1-6), which will securely hold the shrimp while providing for more mobility. The additional shrimp motion afforded by the shrimp harness often will tantalize the more finicky fish into biting. Alternatively, you can get improved mobility without switching to a shrimp harness by removing the treble hooks from the bottom fishing rig and replacing them with #2 **single-barb**, **short-shank** (Shaughnessy) live-bait hooks. Then hook the live shrimp once through the head, being careful not to puncture the dark spot in the center of the head which will kill the shrimp.

Fishing with Lures

There are several artificial baits or **lures** that are effective in the inland waters. Lures are most often used to catch specked trout, white trout, and croakers. Among the most popular lures for the inland waters are the **Mirro lure** and the **grub**, both shown in Figure 1-7. These lures come in many colors, and on any given day, any color may be better than any other. The most productive fishermen will try several colors until they get results. Leaders are not usually necessary, as the sought-after fish usually can't bite through normal fishing line. You simply tie the lure onto your fishing line using the fisherman's knot discussed earlier.

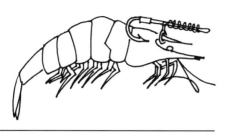

Figure 1-6: The shrimp harness securely holds live shrimp.

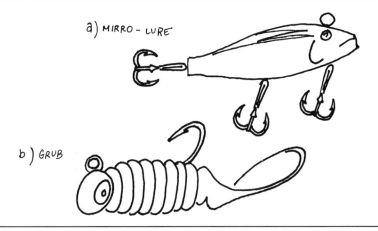

a) MIRRO - LURE

b) GRUB

Figure 1-7: (a) Mirro lure. (b) Grub.

The Mirro lure looks like a small bait fish and has two or three treble hooks. Some Mirro lures are designed to sink (e.g., the 5ZM or TT series) and are designed for deeper water. Other Mirro lures are designed to float on the surface (e.g., the 7M series) and work best in shallow water. Simply cast the lure into any grassy area and slowly wind it in with a gentle jerk of the line about every three or four seconds. When a fish hits, snatch the rod tip toward the sky and begin winding. The treble hooks on the lure usually will hook the fish securely. Land the fish as you would any other.

A grub can be equally effective in the inland waters around the Miracle Strip. It consists of a lead-weighted single hook and a soft jelly-like tail. These tails come in many different colors, so experiment. Hooks from the factory are not always as sharp as they could be so you should sharpen the hook using a wet stone. A sharper hook will hook fish that might otherwise get away. Cast the lure into any grassy area and slowly wind it in with sharp jerks about every two seconds. Again, when you feel a hit, jerk the rod tip toward the sky and wind. When a fish hits your grub, chances are the soft grub tail will be damaged whether you hook the fish or not. You should always fish with an intact grub tail, so have a good supply of extra tails with you. In shallow water, it often helps to put a popping cork in front of a grub and then jerk the cork across the surface of the water as you work the grub. The noise seems to attract fish's attention.

Specializing for Speckled Trout

Speckled trout, also called specks, spotted weakfish, spotted sea trout, and spotted squeteague, are plentiful in the inland waters along the Miracle Strip. You can catch speckled trout year-round, but you have to go to different places depending on the time of year and the temperature. In the winter (mid-November through early March), speckled trout move to deeper water to avoid the temperature fluctuations of shallow water caused by cold fronts. During the winter, fish for speckled trout in the deeper waters of natural holes, man-made canals and channels, or near the entrance of rivers. As the shallow waters are warmed by the spring sun (late March and April), speckled trout, in pursuit of shrimp, will move from deeper water to the grass flats that are commonplace along the shore of Miracle Strip inland waters. Since cold snaps are still common in the spring, try grass flats adjacent to deeper water (the entrance of canals, next to drop-offs, etc.). If the grass flats are not producing on the colder days of spring, try moving back to deeper waters. In the summer, the speckled trout spread throughout the grass flats. Finally, in October and November, they begin to move back to deeper water.

To fish for speckled trout using live shrimp, simply tie a #2 single-barb, short-shank (Shaughnessy) live-bait hook directly onto your line using the fisherman's knot. Then simply hook the shrimp through its head (avoid the dark spot inside the head visible through the shrimp's shell) and you are ready to fish. If a current is running, a small split-shot weight can be attached to the line about twelve inches above the hook. You can also affix a small bobber to the line so you can watch the action as the speckled trout moves in. It is often effective to cast the shrimp up current and let it drift naturally with the current. When a speckled trout takes the live shrimp, give line as necessary for about two full seconds and then quickly start to wind as you snatch the rod tip toward the sky.

During the summer months, pinfish and other smaller fish will often take your live shrimp immediately when you cast out. If this becomes a problem or if live shrimp are not working, switch to a grub or sinking Mirro lure in deeper water or a floating Mirro lure when fishing in the grass flats. The "Fishing with Lures" section earlier in this chapter is directly applicable to fishing for speckled trout.

Where to Go

There are many places that provide inland water fishing access. Just about anywhere you can make a cast and hit the water has the potential of yielding fish. Speckled trout are often found in very shallow water. Water deeper than ten feet with a grassy bottom or near underwater structures is best for other inland water fish. The spots described next are proven to be top fishing spots and can be reached by car or by boat. The number associated with each fishing spot is shown on local maps provided in Appendix B.

#1 Intracoastal Canal

In the Gulf Shores area, the intracoastal waterway narrows into a canal. While fishing from bridges is prohibited here, there is a two-mile section of State Road (SR) 180 (east of the bridge) that provides fishing access to the intracoastal canal. The first bend in SR 180 is known to be a good spot. When parking here, be sure to pull completely off the road and watch out for traffic.

Bottom fishing is the most productive method here. However, the shoreline of the intracoastal canal is lined with rocks. These rocks extend into the water and will snag your line if you aren't careful. To avoid these snags, be sure to wind quickly when pulling in your line. Some fishermen use a bobber to hold their line just off the bottom to avoid snagging on these rocks.

#2 Alabama Point

This is a **pass** (or opening) between island masses that allow boating traffic to navigate between intracoastal waters and the Gulf of Mexico. This pass, also called the Perdido Pass, is located near the Alabama/ Florida state line. A long seawall section on the west side of the pass provides "drive right up" fishing access.

#3 Old Bay Bridge

This is an old concrete bridge three miles in length that used to provide the only link between Pensacola and the Gulf Breeze peninsula (Figure 1-8). It has since been closed to through traffic and is strictly dedicated to fishing. In fact, this is the only bridge in the area that allows fishermen to drive right on, park, and fish right next to the car. Since the middle of the bridge has been removed, there are two separate segments of the Old Bay Bridge: the Gulf Breeze side and the Pensacola side. Each side provides 1 1/2 miles of fishing area over Pensacola Bay. However, as of this writing, only the Gulf Breeze side allows you to drive your car onto the bridge. There is a small fee for fishing on this side of the bridge. There is no fee for fishing on the Pensacola side, but you must park at the foot of the bridge and walk out to your fishing spot. Picnic tables and public restrooms are provided on both sides.

Figure 1-8: The Old Bay Bridge between Pensacola and Gulf Breeze allows fishermen to drive on and fish.

#4 Old Beach Bridge

As with the Old Bay Bridge, the Old Beach Bridge is a two-lane concrete bridge that used to provide a link between Gulf Breeze and Pensacola Beach. When the bridge was retired, the center section was removed, making two separate segments that provide fishing access to the Santa Rosa Sound. There is less fishing space on this bridge than on the Old Bay Bridge; but additional grass beds in the area often make it a better choice for speckled trout fishing. Automobile traffic is not permitted on this bridge but ample parking is available at the foot of either side. Also, there is no fee for fishing on the bridge. There is, however, a toll for crossing the active beach bridge which is necessary to get to the Pensacola Beach side of the Old Beach Bridge.

#5 Ft. Pickens Pier

Near the Pensacola Pass, the Ft. Pickens Pier provides a platform for inland water fishing as well as a chance for some straying Gulf of Mexico species such as king mackerel. Here you can use the bottom fishing techniques described in this chapter as well as some of the surface fishing techniques described in "Chapter 2, "Fishing the Gulf from shore/piers." Swift tidal currents are usually present at the Ft. Pickens Pier because water flows between the Gulf and the inland waters. For this reason, use a heavier weight (e.g., four-ounce pyramid) when bottom fishing here. The pier is in the Ft. Pickens area of the Gulf Islands National Seashore. There is a general admission fee that provides unlimited access to the park facilities. The Ft. Pickens area has miles of undeveloped beaches, picnic areas, museums, fully equipped campgrounds, and a general store. For the nonfishing members of the

Figure 1-9: The East Pass Channel Bridge has walkways suitable for fishing the Choctahatchee Bay.

family, there are lifeguard protected beaches and acres of forts dating back to the early 1800's to explore.

#6 Navarre Bridge

The Navarre Bridge is still actively used as a link between Navarre and Navarre Beach. There is, however, space along the sides of the bridge to safely fish the Santa Rosa Sound. The grassy areas on the Navarre Beach side of the bridge provide speckle trout fishing. There are also adjacent beach areas near the bridge for picnicking. There is a toll for crossing the Navarre Bridge.

#7 East Pass Channel Bridge

Figure 1-9 shows the East Pass Channel Bridge. This active bridge on the way to Destin provides fishing access to the channel that runs between Choctahatchee Bay and the Gulf of Mexico. As with the Navarre Bridge, there is a walkway protected from traffic by a barrier. Bottom fishing techniques work well here. There is an area to park on the west side of the bridge. A nice beach area is located immediately under the bridge on the west side.

#8 Cinco Bayou Bridge

This active bridge in Ft. Walton has an area along each side that provides fishing access to Cinco Bayou. However, there is limited parking and no nearby beach areas. Watch youngsters who fish because the traffic often is heavy.

#9 Garnier Bayou Bridge

Near the Cinco Bayou Bridge, this active bridge also has
a walkway on both sides of the bridge that provides fishing access. The
bottom fishing technique is effective here. There is no fee for fishing on
the bridge, but again, watch the traffic.

#10 Hathaway Bridge

This active bridge in Panama City provides fishing access to the
intracoastal waterway flowing between West Bay and St. Andrews Bay.
Fishing is not allowed on the bridge, but you can park underneath either
end of the bridge and fish from there. Here you fish among the pilings
of the bridge and among the remains of an older bridge next to the active
bridge. Although the water is a little shallow, there are often plenty of
fish to catch. There are no fees for fishing here.

#11 St. Andrews Jetty and Pier

Located in the St. Andrews State Recreation Area, the St. Andrews Jetty
provides for good fishing. This jetty lines the west end of the Panama
City pass. One end of the jetty provides fishing access to the waters in
the channel that flows between St. Andrews Bay and the Gulf of Mexico
(Figure 1-10). The other end of the jetty can serve as a platform for
fishing directly in the Gulf. Bottom fishing is a favorite here. The
adjacent wading area behind the jetty and the large beach areas make this
an ideal place for a family to spend the day. For those who prefer pier
fishing, the recreational area has two piers, one in the Gulf and one on
the north shore that provides fishing access to Grand Lagoon. There is
an admission fee for entry into the St. Andrews State Recreation Area
which provides access to any part of the 1,063-acre recreational area
including boat ramps, nature trails, campgrounds, and picnic areas.

Figure 1-10: The St. Andrews Jetty provides an excellent fishing platform and a nice picnic area.

Chapter

| 2 |

Fishing the Gulf From Shore/Piers

While the inland waters offer good fishing opportunities, the Gulf waters are also accessible to the shore-bound fishermen. The Gulf of Mexico offers a whole new set of fish that can be caught using the techniques covered in this chapter. Fishing can be done from virtually any beach area or from one of the Gulf piers or jetties.

What You Are Likely to Catch

The Gulf of Mexico offers many species of fish that are good to eat. The larger fish found in the Gulf also provide excellent sport fishing for even the most seasoned anglers. Figure 2-1 lists some of the more common catches.

Baits/Rigs/Techniques

When fishing in the Gulf, you have a better chance of catching larger fish. As always, though, almost any fishing tackle can be used to fish the Gulf. The weight of the fishing tackle used is a matter of personal preference. Light tackle for the Gulf might include a light-action rod six feet in length, a medium-sized open-face reel, and 15 lb. test line similar to the setup shown in Figure 1-3. Heavier tackle for fishing the Gulf from shore or from a pier might include a heavier-action 8 foot rod, a larger open-face reel, and 30 lb. test line. Since the larger fish in the Gulf

Type	Eating Quality	Active Periods	Typical Size(lbs.)
King Mackerel	good	May - Nov.	8 to 50
Spanish Mackerel	excellent	March - May	2 to 15
Redfish	excellent	Sept. - April	5 to 40
Sheepshead	good	Sept. - April	2 to 10
Flounder	good	All year	2 to 10
Cobia	excellent	March - June	10 to 80
Tarpon	poor	May - Nov.	50 to 200
Barracuda	poor	May - Nov.	10 to 50
Bluefish	good	Nov. - March	2 to 15
Bonito	poor	April - Nov.	4 to 20
Jack Crevalle	poor	March - Nov.	5 to 50
Whiting	excellent	Oct. - March	1 to 3
Pompano	excellent	March - Nov.	3 to 8

Figure 2-1: Fish commonly caught near shore in the Gulf waters. See Appendix A, "Fish Identification Charts," for drawings of these fish.

tend to run when hooked, make sure whatever reel you have is filled to capacity with line (but not overfilled).

When fishing the Gulf from a pier, you will find yourself some distance above the surface of the water. For this reason, you will have to lift the full weight of the fish you catch from the surface to pier level. Smaller fish can be brought up by grabbing the fishing line with gloved hands and pulling the fish up hand over hand. This is called **hand-lining** the fish. However, larger fish often will be too heavy to lift from the surface of the water with just your fishing line. For this reason, you should have access to a **gaff** when fishing from a Gulf pier. The type of gaff typically used on a pier consists of a rope with a large grappling hook on the end that can be lowered to the water's surface, pulled into a fish, and used to bring the fish up to pier level. Most piers have a gaff available for public use, but you may want to keep a small one in your tackle box just in case.

There are several different techniques for Gulf fishing from shore. Let's take a look at the following techniques:

* Bottom fishing
* Drift fishing
* Cast fishing
* Specializing for redfish

Bottom Fishing

Bottom fishing techniques are exactly the same as those discussed in Chapter 1 under "Bottom fishing" and "Fishing with live shrimp." When used in the Gulf, especially where the surf is breaking, these techniques can yield whiting, pompano, and other excellent tasting fish.

Drift Fishing

The **drift fishing** technique can yield excellent results with a variety of different baits. This technique is fairly simple and often yields king mackerel, Spanish mackerel, and bonito.

The rig used is shown in Figure 2-2. It consists of a length of **steel leader material** as long as the fish you intend to catch, a swivel used to tie the fishing line on and reduce line twisting, and a treble hook. Depending on the type of fish that are around and active, the leader material strength should be 40 lb. test (for Spanish mackerel) or 60 lb. test (for king mackerel). The heavier 60 lb. test leader material is more visible underwater, so smaller Spanish mackerel may be leery. However, the 60 lb. test leader strength is necessary if larger king mackerel are hitting. In general, it is best to use as little hardware as possible since this makes it harder for the fish to see the rig. A black swivel is less visible than a brass swivel and is therefore preferred. A #5 swivel is an appropriate size swivel for king mackerel or Spanish mackerel. The #2 treble hook should be **triple strength** to take the weight of larger fish.

Many times these rigs will be available premade at the tackle shop. Alternatively, you can buy the materials and make your own rigs. If you choose to make your own, you will first need leader material. The noncoated braided steel wire type (e.g., Sevenstrand (R) brand) is fairly easy to work with. You will also need a pair of sharp wire cutters to cut the leader material cleanly. To make your own drift fishing rig, follow these steps:

1. Cut a length of leader material the length of the largest fish you expect to catch. (Thirty-six to forty-eight inches is a good length.)

2. Feed one end of the leader material through the eye of the treble hook and tie an overhand knot. (See Figure 2-3a).

3. Being careful to make a sharp 90-degree bend in the leader material, wrap the leader around itself in a **barrel twist**. Five to seven turns will be sufficient (see Figure 2-3b). It is critical that the bend you make when you twist is a sharp one.

Figure 2-2: Steel leader used for drift fishing.

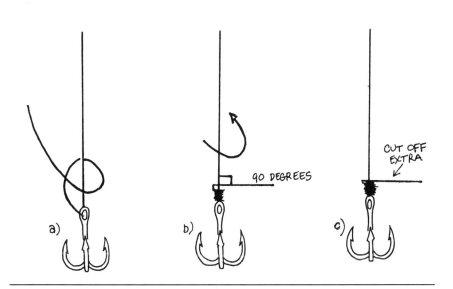

Figure 2-3: Making your own drift fishing rig.

4. Cut of any excess material (see Figure 2-3c).

The swivel is attached to the other end of the leader using the same method.

Once you have your rig, tie it onto the line using the fisherman's knot shown in Figure 1-5.

When drift fishing, you want the bait to be just a few feet below the surface. An ordinary balloon is an easy way to keep your bait fish near the surface and allow you to watch any action develop. Simply blow up a balloon to about five inches in diameter and tie a knot to keep the air in. Then, with a second knot, tie the balloon around the fishing line about five feet above the hook. You are then ready to hook up the bait. You can use either **cigar minnows** or other small fish.

If you can get live cigar minnows, you are more likely to catch fish. However, due to the difficulties of keeping live cigar minnows, tackle shops usually sell them frozen. They should be thawed out before use. Running warm water over them will accelerate this process if necessary. You want the cigar minnow to look as natural as possible so gently move the body from side to side as if the fish were swimming to make the fish more flexible. Then hook one (and only one) of the three treble hook prongs up under the jaw between the gill plates coming out of the top of the nose just in front of the eyes as shown in Figure 2-4a.

If you want to use live cigar minnows, you will have to catch your own, which is a complete art in itself. You can do this by tying a small (#10) gold hook on the line of a light rod and reel. Bait the hook with a small amount of shrimp, squid, or cut bait. Use a small weight (e.g., split shot) if there is a current. Cast the baited hook near the pilings of a pier or near the rocks of a jetty and see what you catch. If cigar minnows are around, you may be able to get a few live ones. If no cigar minnows are around, you may still catch other small bait fish (pinfish, hardtails, etc.). You might want to try these on one of your drift fishing rods.

Still other types of bait fish commonly school up by the thousands around piers and appear to be large black clouds in the water. You can often snatch these fish and use them for bait. To do this, simply cast your unbaited drift fishing rig into the cloud and allow it to settle below the cloud. You will see the cloud part as your rig settles through the school. Within a few seconds, the cloud will close back in around your rig. When this happens, sharply jerk your rod tip toward the sky. If you have snagged one, wind it in and rehook it as discussed next. If not, allow your rig to settle back into the cloud and try again. Although cigar minnows are a top dinner choice among local fish, there is no "best bait" for all situations, so any kind of live bait fish may turn out to be better than fishing with dead cigar minnows.

To hook a live bait fish (cigar minnow or otherwise), simply pass one of the prongs of the treble hook through the back of the fish, as shown in Figure 2-4b. With your rig baited, you are now ready to drift fish. Before you begin to fish, you must set the reel's **drag**. The drag is designed to automatically dispense line as you are fighting a fish before the breaking point of the line is reached. This prevents a strong fish from breaking the line. The drag should be set to yield line well before the breaking point of the line is reached. Most fish caught using this technique will break the line if the drag is set too tight. If the drag is too loose, however, you will not be able to properly hook or fight the fish. A little experimenting is necessary to find the right setting.

Give the cigar minnow a good cast down current and allow it to seek its own level. Leave the reel **free spooled** meaning that line can freely flow off the reel. Prevent further line from being released by lightly holding the line with your fingers. *Do not wrap the line around your finger or it could be injured if a large fish takes the line.*

When a fish takes the bait, it will start to "run," pulling the line from your

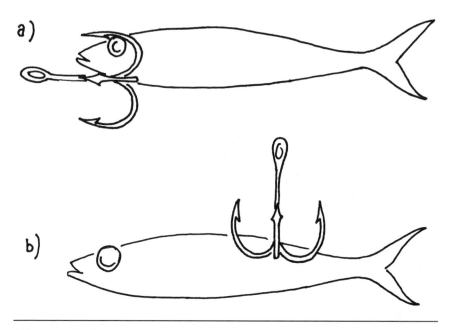

Figure 2-4: Hooking bait fish. a) Hooking a dead bait fish. b) Hooking a live bait fish.

loose finger grip. The reel will then allow the fish to take line without any tension as you point the rod toward the fish. The fish's movement will usually cause the balloon to pop, so it will no longer provide resistance when dragging through the water.

At this point it is important to let the fish have line so that it doesn't feel any tension for a full count of four (one thousand one, one thousand two, etc.). This gives the fish time to swallow the bait. Once you have finished counting, quickly begin to wind the reel, which will stop the line from freely feeding out, and strongly snatch the rod tip up toward the sky several times. Continue to hold tension in the line at all times by keeping the rod tip up and constantly winding the reel, allowing the drag to determine your progress.

After the hook is well set, stop winding but continue to hold the rod tip toward the sky. If the fish is running and pulling out line against your drag, let it. This is what you want to happen. The fish is working very hard and will soon tire. Once the running stops, wind the reel as you slowly lower the tip of the rod toward the fish, being careful not to give any slack in the line. When the rod tip is almost pointing at the fish, stop reeling and gently pull the rod tip back toward the sky. Continue this pumping action (reeling the tip down and then pulling it back toward the sky) to work the fish toward you. Let the fish get fully exhausted and under your control before trying to land it. If you are on a pier and the fish is too large to lift without breaking your line, use a gaff (described earlier).

Cast Fishing

Cast fishing is a minor variation of drift fishing that is most effective from a pier. You will catch basically the same type of fish. You use the same rig as with drift fishing (see Figure 2-2) and similarly, you use a dead cigar minnow hooked through the nose as bait (see Figure 2-3a). The primary difference between drift fishing and cast fishing is that with cast fishing you actively cast the bait and slowly wind it back to you with a gentle jerk of the rod (about once per second).

While this technique takes more effort, it makes the cigar minnow appear to be swimming through the water, resulting in a more natural appearance. Remember, the more natural the bait looks, the better.

This technique can be done most effectively on a pier rather than from the shore for two reasons. First, you can cast greater distances from a pier because the added height above the water enlarges the area you can cover. Second, the elevation of a pier (along with some good **polarized** sunglasses) will allow you to see into the water and actually spot fish. Rather than blindly casting your bait over and over again (which can, by the way, provide good results), you may choose to wait until you see a fish before casting. When you spot a fish, which appears as a shadow swiftly moving along, then cast your bait a little (e.g., twenty feet) in front of the fish so that your cigar minnow has a little time to sink before the fish arrives.

This is a very exciting way to fish since you can watch the drama unfold as the fish hopefully turns toward your bait and frantically eats it. When you see or feel this happen, you perform the same steps just described for "Drift fishing," including freely feeding line to the fish for a full four seconds before setting the hook (stopping the line and snatching the rod). As you might expect, accurately casting in front of swiftly moving fish will test your casting proficiency. You should also be aware that there will usually be other people cast fishing right beside you for those same fish. While this can make for very exciting fishing, the less aggressive fisherman may not enjoy this competitive environment and may choose other fishing techniques.

Specializing for Redfish

Redfish, also called red drum or channel bass, are a favorite quarry along the Gulf Coast. While you might catch a redfish at any time during the year, the best time to specialize for this fish is in the fall and early winter (September through December). This is when the redfish collect in schools and migrate from east to west along the Gulf Coast. Smaller redfish are under five pounds, while the larger fish (called sow redfish) can easily be over thirty pounds.

Since redfish are fairly large and quite strong, either a large open-face reel with 30 lb. test line and a heavy-action casting rod or a conventional reel with 40 lb. test line and a heavy action rod is appropriate. The grouper rig shown in Figure 3-5 in the next chapter is an effective style of rig when you specialize for Redfish. However, for Redfish use a

5/0 hook, an 80 lb. test monofilament leader (25 inches long), and an eight ounce egg weight (twelve ounces in a heavy current). Live bait such as menhaden, pinfish, and croakers work best. Menhaden collect in large schools and start entering the inland waters around August. They can usually be seen from the surface and can be caught with a cast net. Pinfish and croakers can be caught in traps or using a version (with small single hooks) of the bottom rig shown in Figure 1-4. Alternately, you can buy frozen menhaden and cut them in half or strips of cut mullet for bait.

The best places to go after redfish are in the passes (listed here and in Chapters 3) between inland waterways and the Gulf of Mexico. Many like to go after redfish at night, but persistence can pay off any time of day. You can fish from the beach (surf fishing rod holders are recommended) or from a bridge if available. Cast out into deep water and let the bait rest on the bottom. Keep the drag very loose or free-spooled using the reel's "clicker" or a rubber band around the line and rod just in front of the reel to hold the line. When the rod tip begins to bounce, pick up the rod and feed the fish line as needed for about ten full seconds. Then wind up the slack and strongly jerk the rod tip up toward the sky as you continue to wind.

Where to Go

There are many fishing spots along the beaches of the Miracle Strip that provide access to the Gulf of Mexico. Fishing in the surf line anywhere along the beach can provide good results using the bottom fishing techniques described in Chapter 1. Pompano and whiting are commonly caught bottom fishing from the beach in this manner. The wave action along the beach and the slowly sloping bottom usually make drift fishing or cast fishing from the beach difficult at best. The Gulf piers and jetties provide good platforms for bottom fishing as well as the other techniques described in this chapter. King mackerel, Spanish mackerel, tarpon, jack crevalle, and similar fish are more likely to be caught from the Gulf piers. Some of the prime locations for fishing the Gulf from beaches, piers, and jetties are discussed next.

#12 West Pass

This small pass is the only connection between Little Lagoon and the Gulf of Mexico. In fact, other than this pass, the Little Lagoon is completely isolated from any other body of water. The sea wall located here provides limited access to the Gulf of Mexico. While many types of fishing can be done here, it is best suited for bottom fishing in the surf line.

Figure 2-5: Pensacola Beach Fishing Pier.

Fish traffic flowing between Little Lagoon and the Gulf of Mexico must travel through this pass. Public parking is provided along with public restrooms. Adjacent beach areas make for good picnicking.

#13 Alabama State Fishing Pier

The concrete fishing pier in Gulf Shores is part of Alabama's park system. It provides fishing access into the Gulf of Mexico. There is a small usage fee for those fishing or even just looking. Limited public parking is provided adjacent to clean beach areas for the nonfishing members of the family. Any of the fishing techniques discussed in this chapter can be used here.

#14 Pensacola Beach Fishing Pier

This wooden pier is located in the heart of Pensacola Beach near shopping and lifeguard-protected beaches (see Figure 2-5). It provides an excellent platform for any of the fishing techniques discussed in this chapter and consistently produces good catches. There is a fee for fishing or just looking. There are lifeguard-protected beaches, shops, and restaurants adjacent to the pier.

#15 Navarre Beach Fishing Pier

This fishing pier is located at Navarre Beach and lends itself to all fishing techniques discussed in this chapter. While Navarre Beach is less developed than Pensacola Beach, there are a few beach shops and restaurants nearby. Lifeguard-protected beaches surround the pier. There is a fee for fishing on this pier.

#16 Okaloosa Island Pier

This concrete pier in the heart of Ft. Walton Beach provides plenty of good fishing. Again, shopping, restaurants, and hotels surround the area. This, plus adjacent beaches, allows those not fishing to have fun. All techniques can be effective on this pier. There is fee for fishing or observing.

#17 East Pass Jetties

For those willing to make a hike, there is excellent fishing to be had here. These are rocks that line the east and west side of the East Pass connecting the Gulf of Mexico with the inland waters near Destin. While this spot lends itself best to bottom fishing techniques, drift and cast fishing techniques can work during an outgoing tide. The jetties on the east side are the most accessible in that you can park closer to them. Further, the east side provides easier access to the Gulf waters as far as rock climbing is concerned. To get to the west side, it is best to park at the west end of the East Pass Channel Bridge. The hike to the west side is farther, and once you get there you need be more nimble footed to climb out on the rocks that make up the jetty. Either side offers nice beach areas for picnicking. There are no restaurants or shops, so bring a lunch.

#18 Dan Russell Pier

This Gulf pier is the longest fishing pier on Panama City Beach (see Figure 2-6). It provides an excellent fishing platform for any of the fishing techniques discussed in this chapter. Adjacent beach areas, shopping, and restaurants offer something for everyone. There is a fee for fishing or observing.

Figure 2-6: The Dan Russell Pier on Panama City Beach.

#19 Bay County Pier

This Gulf pier is located in the heart of Panama City Beach. There is no fee for fishing on this pier, but it is shorter than most Gulf piers. It makes an excellent platform for bottom fishing along the surf line. Nice beaches stretch for miles in either direction, as do shops and restaurants.

#20 St. Andrews Jetty and Gulf Pier

Located in the St. Andrews State Recreation Area, the St. Andrews jetty provides for good fishing. This jetty lines the west end of the Panama City pass. The southern end of the jetty line provides access for Gulf fishing. There usually are strong currents along the outer side of the jetties, so use heavier weights (four ounce pyramids) when bottom fishing here. This area lends itself to bottom fishing, but with an outgoing tide, drift and cast fishing are possible. On the inside of the jetty, there is a natural wading pool with a sandy beach excellent for casual swimming. This, plus nearby grilling and picnicking areas, makes for a complete family outing.

For those who prefer pier fishing, the recreational area has two piers, one in the Gulf and one on the north shore that provides fishing access to Grand Lagoon. The Gulf pier, however, is quite short, making it best used as a platform for fishing the surf line.

There is an admission fee that provides access to any part of the 1,063 acre recreational area including boat ramps, nature trails, campgrounds, and picnic areas.

Chapter

3

Fishing the Gulf from a Boat

With a boat, you have access to the best fishing the Gulf of Mexico has to offer. While much good fishing can be had from shore, a boat offers access to deeper water and underwater structures that attract bait fish and their inevitable predators. While there are some natural reef structures, most of the more popular fishing spots are artificial reefs (e.g., sunken ships, barges, or bridge rubble). Before we get into fishing the Gulf by boat, let's pause to cover some safety information.

Local Boating Safety Information

The Gulf of Mexico offers clear, warm, and usually calm waters that can provide many days of safe boating and excellent fishing. As with boating anywhere, though, safety is of primary importance. The U.S. Coast Guard offers safe-boating classes all over the country that will help teach you basic boating safety. The classes are highly recommended either as an introduction to new boaters or as a refresher for old salts.

In addition, safe boating requires knowledge about the local area in which you intend to operate. While complete boating safety information is beyond the scope of this book, following are some safety tips related to the area.

Weather Patterns

The weather around the Miracle Strip is often difficult to predict. Especially in the summer, thunderstorms are common and can quickly develop, catching boaters by surprise. For this reason, boaters should frequently check the weather reports that are broadcast 24 hours a day on VHF radio channels 1, 2, and 3. What appears to be a sunny and calm day can quickly become filled with intense localized thunderstorms spawning water spouts. As always, use good judgment. Know where you are in relation to the closest pass at all times and don't venture beyond the safe range of your boat or experience. For smaller boats, there is plenty of good fishing in inland waters and in the Gulf waters immediately around passes.

Since the summers in this area are both hot and humid, be sure to keep plenty of water on board. A good way to do this is to fill plastic milk jugs with water and freeze them the night before the trip. You can use these frozen jugs in ice chests to keep your fish and food cool while having reserve water when they thaw.

Another necessity for spending a day in the Gulf (or inland waters, for that matter) is shade. The hot sun will quickly overheat an unprotected fisherman as well as produce an intense sunburn. Even a simple Bimini top can provide the refuge from the sun necessary for spending extended periods on a boat. However, don't underestimate the effects of sun rays reflected off the water. These rays can burn exposed skin and eyes even while you are in the shade! Invest in some potent sun-blocking lotion, sunglasses (polarized sunglasses will let you see into the water better), and a hat with a brim.

While fishing is still good (and sometimes better) in the winter, frequent north winds often make the Gulf waters rough. (In other words, there are fewer calm days in the winter than in the summer.) Further, the cold winds can quickly chill an exposed fisherman, especially when dampened by 50-degree sea spray. For these reasons, winter boating typically requires a larger boat to handle the larger seas and provide protection from the cold.

Passes

Inland waters provide access to the Gulf of Mexico through the passes between island masses. Strong currents are frequently found in these areas as large quantities of water shift due to tidal actions. These strong currents along with tidal actions tend to frequently shift the bottom profiles in these areas, usually causing shallow regions on either side of the pass. Watch for these areas which will cause waves to shoal and make for a boating hazard. Further, wave action often is stronger in the area of a pass due to currents, bottom irregularities, and other boating traffic. If you are not familiar with navigating such passes or if you are new to the area, you may want to watch a few other boats go through the pass before you make your way.

One other notable feature near the Pensacola Pass is a sunken battleship, the USS Massachusetts (USS Mass). This ship makes for a good fishing reef, but it also is a safety hazard since the ship's gun turrets are just barely awash. More than one unaware skipper has hit the USS Mass causing severe damage to his vessel (not to the USS Mass). It is located about a mile and a half south of the Pensacola Pass just west of the shipping channel. It is marked by buoy WR2.

Diver-Down Flags

Skin and SCUBA divers are required by law to display a **diver-down flag** while diving. There are two types of diver-down flags. One is a red square with a white diagonal stripe; the other is a blue and white flag.

When you see a diver-down flag, reduce your speed and exercise extreme caution as surfacing divers may be difficult to see in the water.

What If You Have Trouble?

Every year there are boaters that find themselves stranded in the Gulf of Mexico in need of assistance. These boaters might have engine failures or electrical failures or might have simply run out of gas. In any case, the U.S. Coast Guard is always ready to provide assistance.

If you find yourself stranded in the Gulf, first anchor your vessel (if possible) to prevent drifting further from shore, to more isolated areas, or into breaking surf. Then try to contact the Coast Guard on VHF channel 16. This channel is to be used exclusively for distress calls or hailing other vessels. Use a message such as "Coast Guard Station Pensacola, this is the [name of your vessel]. Over" The Coast Guard will ask you to switch to another channel (probably Coast Guard working VHF channels 21, 23, or 81). They will want information such as your position, the nature of your distress, the number of people on board, and so forth. If necessary, they will dispatch a Coast Guard vessel to meet you and tow you to a nearby port.

While a VHF radio is strongly recommended anytime you venture into the Gulf of Mexico, electrical failures can make them useless. Some boaters carry a spare hand-held VHF radio as a backup. If you are unable to communicate via radio for whatever reason, you should try to flag down any vessels in the area by waving a bright rag or shirt and sounding your horn, bell, or whistle. The other vessel may be able to tow you to port or call the Coast Guard for you. If you are unable to hail another vessel, your last resort is to fire flares to attract attention. Anytime you are stranded in the Gulf, the situation should be taken seriously and action should be taken promptly.

Type	Eating Quality	Active Periods	Typical Size(lbs.)
King Mackerel	good	May - Nov.	8 to 50
Spanish Mackerel	excellent	March - May	2 to 15
Redfish	excellent	Sept. - April	5 to 40
Trigger Fish	excellent	All Year	1 to 15
Amberjack	excellent	Nov. - May	18 to 90
Cobia	excellent	March - June	10 to 80
Tarpon	poor	May - Nov.	50 to 200
Barracuda	poor	May - Nov.	10 to 50
Bluefish	good	Nov. - March	2 to 15
Bonito	poor	April - Nov.	4 to 20
Jack Crevalle	poor	March - Nov.	5 to 50
Wahoo	excellent	May - Nov.	15 to 45
Red Snapper	excellent	All year	3 to 30
Grouper	excellent	All year	10 to 65
Dolphin	excellent	May - Nov.	2 to 45

Figure 3-1: Fish commonly caught while fishing in the Gulf from a boat. See "APPENDIX A: Fish identification charts" for drawings of these fish.

What You Are Likely to Catch

When fishing from a boat, you have the added advantage of reaching deeper water and various underwater structures that are home to many large and tasty fish. Figure 3-1 lists some of the more common catches.

Baits/Rigs/Techniques

A boat is an excellent platform for a variety of fishing techniques. Since there are more large fish found in the deeper Gulf waters accessible by boat, heavier fishing tackle is usually in order. Due to the flexibility offered by boat fishing, more decisions have to be made about the type of fishing you want to do. While the same tackle can be used for almost any type of fishing, some equipment is better suited to a particular technique than another. Additional equipment necessary for the boating Gulf fisherman is a hand gaff and fishing gloves. The gaff used from a boat consists of a handle or pole with a large hook attached to the end. This gaff is used to lift an exhausted fish from the surface of the water and into your boat. Without a gaff, you would have to hand-line the fish into the boat by grabbing the fishing line with gloved hands and pulling. For larger fish, this could result in pulling out the hook or breaking the line, either of which will lose the fish for you. The fishing gloves help protect your hands from line burns, sharp fins, and so forth.

Landing a large fish is a two-person operation. As the fisherman works the exhausted fish toward the boat, the gaffer puts on work gloves to protect his or her hands. Then the gaffer grabs the fishing line loosely with one hand and pulls the fish into reach. With the other hand, the gaffer positions the gaff hook under the fish. With one smooth motion, the gaffer pulls the gaff up and into the fish's midsection and then directly into the boat.

Many Gulf fish have very sharp teeth (e.g., king mackerel) that can inflict a nasty bite. *Never put your hands into a fish's mouth for any reason.* Even after a fish has been out of the water for a good while and appears to be motionless, it may still have enough life left to suddenly snap its jaws. Use pliers and gloves when removing hooks from the fish's mouth.

With this understanding, let's examine the following fishing techniques that are known to be productive when fishing the Gulf by boat:

       * Bottom fishing
       * Drift fishing
       * Cast fishing
       * Trolling

Bottom Fishing

Of all the techniques discussed in this chapter, bottom fishing is the most reliable way to ensure you don't come back empty-handed. This, along with the fact that it is also one of the simplest techniques to learn, makes it a good place for the beginner to start. The local favorites, red snapper, grouper, and amberjack are caught using this technique. The most important thing when bottom fishing in the Gulf is to make sure you are over some type of irregularity in the bottom such as a shipwreck or rocks. These types of underwater irregularities provide a platform for the growth of underwater organisms that provide food for small bait fish. As these bait fish collect, they attract larger fish which feed on the bait fish. Since most of the Gulf bottom is barren sand, randomly anchoring over any old spot is a sure way to decrease your odds of catching fish when bottom fishing. The "Where to Go" section of this chapter will help you anchor at a good spot.

While almost any type of tackle can be used, the larger fish you are likely to encounter while bottom fishing the Gulf will require heavy tackle.

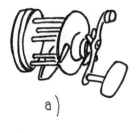

a)

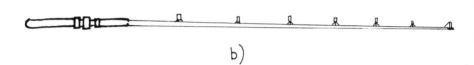

b)

Figure 3-2: Heavy-weight tackle used for bottom fishing in the Gulf. a) Conventional reel. b) Boat rod.

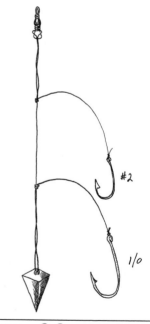

You will be fishing near shipwrecks and rock piles, and the bottom fish that live there are very good at entangling your line once they are hooked. When a fish is hooked, it is a natural reaction for it to swim frantically through the wreck or structure seeking safety and dragging your fishing line with it. Nothing is more frustrating than finally hooking the "big one," only to have your line quickly cut by a piece of scrap metal on the bottom.

The way to avoid this problem is to pull the fish off the bottom as quickly as you can. Especially for larger bottom fish, this requires a heavy rod, heavy line, and a strong reel all de-

Figure 3-3: Bottom rig used for Gulf fishing from a boat.

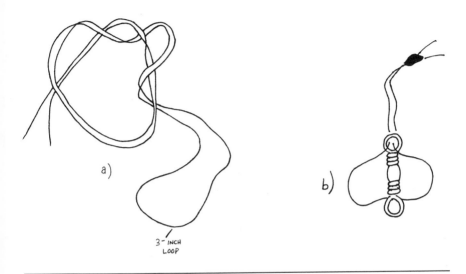

a)

3-INCH
LOOP

b)

Figure 3-4: Making a bottom rig.

signed for bottom fishing (see Figure 3-2).

The type of rig used for this type of bottom fishing is shown in Figure 3-3. Since many bottom fish (especially red snapper and grouper) can see quite well, it is important to make the rig as invisible as possible. For this reason, heavy monofilament line (not steel leader material) is used to make the rig. Tackle stores sell similar rigs ready made or you can make your own with a little practice. The rig is made of 60 lb. test monofilament line. To make a heavy rig for bottom fishing, follow these steps:

1. Pick up the spool of 60 lb. text monofilament line and find the loose end. Make a three-inch loop by tying a double overhand knot about eighteen inches from the end (see Figure 3-4a).

2. Pass this loop through the eye of the swivel and then around the swivel (see Figure 3-4b).

3. Tie a #2 hook onto the remaining loose end using the fisherman's knot (see Figure 3-3).

4. Tie a five-inch loop twelve inches below the first knot, again using a double overhand knot. Place a four-ounce pyramid weight on this loop by passing the loop through the eye of the weight as with the swivel in step 2 (see Figure 3-4b).

6. Cut the remaining end to be twelve inches long and use a fisherman's knot to tie on a 1/0 hook.

After you have made a few rigs, you will be able to make them very quickly. Tie the rig onto your line using the fisherman's knot and you are ready to fish.

The baits used for bottom fishing in the Gulf include cigar minnows

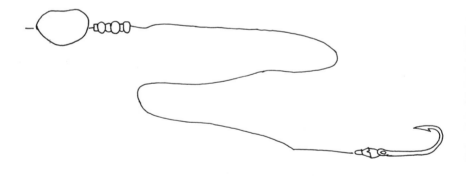

Figure 3-5: Rig used for grouper fishing in the deeper Gulf waters.

(sometimes whole, sometimes cut into halves or thirds), squid, shrimp, or other cut bait. Put the point of the hook through the bait at least two times and make sure that the barb is exposed. Then lower the baited rig down to the bottom and wind up two turns of the reel. Point the rod tip down toward the water and wait. When you feel a strike, snatch the rod up toward the sky and begin to wind the reel. If you feel that you have hooked the fish, pull it a few feet off the bottom as quickly as possible to avoid becoming entangled or cut off. Then allow the fish to tire as you consistently work it toward the surface. When the fish reaches the surface, it can be hand-lined or gaffed as necessary.

When fishing the deeper Gulf waters (around 80 feet deep and deeper) where large grouper and other fish are commonly found, another rig (see Figure 3-5) often is used. Since grouper can also be "spooked" by steel leader material, heavy monofilament line is used. Again, this rig may be purchased or easily made. Follow these steps to make this rig:

1. Cut a length of 60 or 80 lb. test monofilament line 48 to 60 inches long.

2. Using the fisherman's knot (but with only four or five turns), tie a #5 swivel on one end and a 3/0 hook on the other.

3. Thread your fishing line through an **egg weight** (8 to 16 ounces) and then tie your line to the swivel using the fisherman's knot.

With this rig, a whole cigar minnow is used. Dead cigar minnows are hooked through the nose and live cigar minnows are hooked through the tail (see Figure 2-4). Since the line freely feeds through the egg weight, this rig lets larger fish take line without feeling the weight, giving them time to swallow the cigar minnow.

After you bait the rig, make sure the drag is set so that the reel will give line before the breaking point is reached. Now lower the rig to the bottom slowly to avoid getting the rig twisted around itself. Once the weight is on the bottom, leave the reel disengaged and stop line from running off the reel by resting your thumb on the line. Now you wait.

When a fish takes the bait, feed it line for a full count of five (one thousand one, one thousand two, etc.). Then lock the reel, snatch the rod toward the sky, and wind. Try to get the fish a few feet off the bottom as quickly as possible to avoid having your line cut on any bottom structures. Once you are some distance off the bottom, allow the fish to tire before bringing it to the surface. Then, depending on the size of the fish, either hand-line the fish into the boat or gaff it.

Drift Fishing

Drift fishing from a boat in the Gulf is exactly the same as drift fishing from a pier. (See the section on drift fishing in chapter 2.) Since you won't have a need to pull a fish off the bottom, you don't need the heavy tackle needed for bottom fishing the Gulf from a boat. However, as with bottom fishing, you will usually have the best luck near bottom irregularities since these attract bait fish which attract larger fish. King mackerel, Spanish mackerel, barracuda, cobia, and bonito are among the most common catches for this type of fishing.

Cast Fishing

Cast fishing from a boat is the same as cast fishing from a pier. (See the section on cast fishing in Chapter 2.) The primary difference is that since you usually don't have the elevation above the surface offered by a pier, it is more difficult to spot fish. For this reason, most cast fishermen blindly cast over underwater structures or near surface structures found in the Gulf such as buoys or the exposed portions of the USS Mass. The same types of fish caught using the drift fishing technique can also be caught in this manner.

Trolling

Trolling is another fishing alternative that is popular in the local Gulf waters. With this fishing technique, baits or lures are dragged behind a boat slowly making way. Favorite catches of the trolling fisherman include king mackerel, Spanish mackerel, wahoo, and bonito.

The advantages of the trolling technique include covering a large area and giving the bait or lure forward motion, making it look more natural. Disadvantages of trolling include increased gas consumption, noise from the engines, and the need for a full-time helmsman.

The type of tackle used can be either of the types shown in Figure 1-3 and Figure 3-2 depending on how much of a fight you want to have on

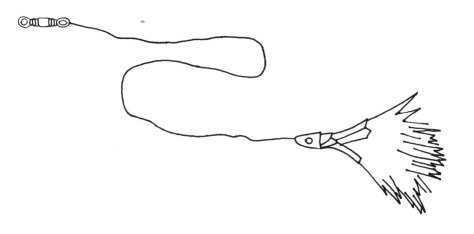

Figure 3-6: Rig used for trolling in the Gulf waters.

your hands. There are many different types of trolling lures and rigs used in the local waters. One of the most productive rigs is shown in Figure 3-6. It consists of a swivel, some steel leader, a **feather duster**, and a cigar minnow harness. The steel leader is necessary because the mackerel commonly caught trolling can easily bite through regular fishing line. The feather duster is the lure and a cigar minnow is usually put on behind the feather duster as shown in Figure 3-7.

This rig can be purchased ready to use or can be made by the fisherman. To make this rig, you will need a #5 swivel, the feather duster lure (red and white and blue and white lures are effective), some 60 lb. test uncoated-steel leader material, a cigar minnow harness, and a good pair of wire cutters.

Figure 3-7: A cigar minnow is trailed behind the feather duster by using a cigar minnow harness.

1. Cut a length of leader material the length of the largest fish you expect to catch. (48 to 60 inches is a good rule of thumb for trolling.)

2. Feed one end of the leader material through the eye of the cigar minnow harness and tie an overhand knot followed by a barrel twist as shown in Figure 2-3. As before, make a sharp 90-degree bend in the leader material when making the barrel twist. (Five to seven wraps will be sufficient.) Practice until you can wrap the harness end of the leader correctly.

3. Slide the leader material through the feather duster and attach a small black swivel to the other end of the leader material using the same overhand knot followed by a barrel roll.

4. Sharpen the hook using a wet stone.

Once you have your rig, tie it onto the line using the fisherman's knot. You are now ready to hook the cigar minnow onto the rig. You want the cigar minnow to look as natural as possible, so make sure it is completely thawed and gently move the body from side to side as if the fish were swimming to make the fish more flexible. Then attach the cigar minnow to the harness following the instructions provided with the harness.

Check the drag setting of the reel to ensure that line will be fed out long before the breaking point of the line is reached, but with enough tension to allow you to set the hook. Most fish caught using this technique will break the line if the drag is set too tight.

As the boat makes way at two or three knots (speed is not that critical), dip the baited feather duster into the water just beside the boat for a few seconds and watch how it trails against the boat's motion. It is critical that you make sure the rig is not spinning. You will limit your chances of catching a fish if your bait is spinning since this doesn't look very natural. Common causes of spinning baits are partially frozen (i.e., bent) cigar minnows or improper attachment of the cigar minnow to the harness. Check these things and if it is still spinning, try gently slapping the rig against the surface of the water a few times or switching cigar minnows.

Once the bait is trailing correctly, feed it out 30 to 50 yards behind the boat. (The distance you let it out is not critical.) Double check the drag setting of the reel, place the rod in the rod holder, and you are trolling. When trolling with multiple rods, be sure to put the lines out at different distances to help prevent them from getting entangled. Also, make wide gradual turns when trolling to avoid tangles. You may also want to use a **planer** on one or more of your lines, which allows you to troll a line deeper than normal. Since fish may be hanging at any depth on any given day, trolling a deep line or two may pay off.

Check the lines frequently to ensure the baits are intact and that there is no seaweed on the line. When a fish hits a trolling line, the reel will sing out. When this happens, quickly pick up the rod being careful not to give the fish any slack. There is usually no need to set the hook (snatch the rod) since the forward motion of the boat has already done that. Continue to hold tension in the line at all times by keeping the rod tip up and winding the reel to remove any slack that develops. If the fish is running and pulling out line against your drag, let it go. This is what you want to happen. The fish is working very hard and will soon tire. Once the running stops, wind the reel as you slowly lower the tip of the rod toward the fish, being careful not to give any slack in the line. When the rod tip is pointed almost directly toward the fish, stop reeling and pull the rod tip gently back toward the sky. Continue this pumping action (reeling the tip down and then pulling the tip back toward the sky) to work the fish toward you. Let the fish get fully exhausted and under your control before trying to land it. After the fish is completely exhausted, hand-line or gaff the fish as necessary.

Where to Go

When preparing to troll or drift fish in the Gulf waters, you can get many different answers to the question, "Where is the best place to go?" Some fishermen will stop right in the pass or just any old place in the Gulf and start fishing. Others will run twenty miles or farther offshore before putting out their lines. On any given day, either approach might be the correct one. Since the fish you normally catch trolling and drift fishing are always on the move, you are liable to catch fish anywhere you might find yourself in the Gulf. Some things that can improve your trolling luck include fishing over and around free-floating weed lines, near the artificial reefs listed later in this section, or around buoys. Since all of these attract small bait fish, they also attract larger fish that feed on the bait fish.

For bottom fishing, finding a good reef is vital and can make the difference between catching your limit or going home empty-handed. Organisms grow on the reefs providing food for smaller fish. As these smaller fish accumulate, the larger fish come to feed on them. A natural food chain is developed around the reef providing for good bottom fishing. Since most of the Gulf bottom around the reefs is barren sand, a distance of a dozen yards can make all the difference in the world.

There are many reefs within reach of the properly equipped boater that consistently provide good fishing. Most of these spots are artificial reefs. These reefs might consist of boxcars, ships, washing machines, or the concrete rubble from an old bridge. These things are intentionally dumped into the Gulf at predefined locations just to make reefs, which is good for the environment and good for fishing and SCUBA diving.

Since most of the reefs are several miles from shore, navigational equipment is most helpful in finding them. Ideally, you should be equipped with a LORAN and a fathometer. The LORAN, which stands for Long-Range Aid to Navigation, tracks radio signals from land-based LORAN stations and triangulates your position quite accurately. The fathometer maps the profile of the bottom as your vessel moves over it allowing you to pinpoint irregularities (such as reefs). For those equipped with a LORAN and a fathometer, the table starting on the facing page gives the LORAN coordinates for many popular fishing spots.

For those without electronics, the approximate compass headings and distances can be plotted on navigational charts using the LORAN coordinates given. A compass heading and distance alone is sufficient to find the USS Mass for example, which is near the Pensacola Pass. This sunken battleship is partially awash and is marked with a buoy (WR2). This wreck can provide excellent fishing (especially drift and cast fishing) and can easily be found. As new artificial reefs are built offshore, they often are marked with buoys for a period of time. Check the most current navigational charts to see what buoys are still maintained. Another alternative for bottom fishermen is to go to the rock jetties that line all of the passes along the Miracle Strip. These jetties are easily found and offer good bottom fishing.

Finally, there is one other method available to boaters without electronics. On weekends or holidays when the weather is nice, the most popular spots will be populated with a number of fishing boats. If you anchor near the cluster of boats, you should be on or near enough to a reef to catch fish if they are biting. However, when using this approach, you should have a backup plan in case you can't find a crowd.

#	Reef	LOP #1	LOP #2	Notes
21.	Buffalo Barge #1	12881.9	47045.5	54' deep, 21 miles from Perdido Pass
22.	Buffalo Barge #2	12876.8	47044.3	66' deep, 20 miles from Perdido Pass
23.	Morgan Pipes	12883.1	47040.0	66' deep, 21 miles from Perdido Pass
24.	Lipscomb Tug	13151.0	47050.2	65' deep, 19 miles from Perdido Pass
25.	105' Tug	12957.8	47039.9	64' deep, 17 miles from Perdido Pass
26.	Liberty Ship Sparkman	12948.1	47020.2	93 ' deep, 20 miles from Perdido Pass
27.	Lillian Bridge	13046.7	47062.8	60' deep, 11 miles from Perdido Pass
28.	Liberty Ship Allen	13069.4	47046.4	88' deep, 10 miles from Perdido Pass
29.	Lillian Bridge 2	13059.2	47054.9	92' deep, 11 miles from Perdido Pass
30.	Liberty Ship Wallace	13037.4	47046.4	90' deep, 13 miles from Perdido Pass
31.	Mobil Oil Platform	13070.0	47020.0	96' deep, 18 miles from Perdido Pass
32.	Trysler Grounds	13080.0	46995.0	102' deep, 22 miles from Perdido Pass
33.	USS Mass			30' deep, near P'cola Pass (see note 1)

#	Reef	LOP #1	LOP #2	Notes
34.	Russian Freightor	13263.8	47077.1	80' deep, 9 miles from Pensacola Pass
35.	Green's Hole	13279.8	47061.7	116' deep
36.	Bridge Rubble	13277.5	47091.9	80' deep, 8 miles from Pensacola Pass
37.	21 Hole	13248.2	47027.2	126' deep
38.	3 Barges	13270.7	47107.8	45' deep
39.	Bucks Place	13334.4	47072.5	105' deep
40.	P5M Airplane	13325.6	47106.4	85' deep, 10 miles from Pensacola Pass
41.	1/2 Barge	13202.0	47086.1	60' deep
42.	Rock Cliffs	13464.7	47040.9	160' deep, 27 miles from Pensacola Pass
43.	Tenneco Rig	13323.0	47013.0	175' deep, 22 miles from P'cola Pass
44.	Liberty Ship (J. Meek)	13306.8	47102.5	67' deep
45.	Tex Edwards Barge	13300.4	47101.9	63' deep, 8 miles from P'cola Pass

#	Reef	LOP #1	LOP #2	Notes
46.	Airplane	13279.0	47049.2	88' deep
47.	Tessie	13250.2	47078.7	75' deep, 9 miles from P'cola Pass
48.	Casino Reef	13333.3	47115.0	60' deep, 11 miles from P'cola Pass
49.	Brown Barge	13660.7	47134.1	68' deep, 6 miles from Destin Pass
50.	Pole Spot	13720.4	47131.0	70' deep, 4 miles from Destin Pass
51.	Rock Bottom	13730.5	47130.6	80' deep, 5 miles from Destin Pass
52.	Concrete Piles	13767.5	47136.6	70' deep, 7 miles from Destin Pass
53.	C'mas Tree Reef	13768.4	47136.5	40-70' deep, tires and concrete
54.	Liberty Ship	13511.4	47101.4	70' deep
55.	Big Amberjack	13476.0	47073.9	110' deep, 10' relief
56.	Coral Reef	13738.4	47041.5	115' deep, 19 miles from Destin Pass
57.	Flats	13550.0	46975.0	375' deep, 31 miles from Destin Pass
58.	Grey Ghost	13891.1	46991.7	106' deep, 19 miles from P. City Pass

#	Reef	LOP #1	LOP #2	Notes
59.	Smith Barge	14066.9	46976.0	
60.	Holland Barge	14065.7	46981.1	
61.	Blown-up Barge	14052.4	46992.5	
62.	Offshore Twin	14067.7	46967.0	
63.	Inshore Twin	14069.0	46968.0	
64.	Longbeach Barge	14067.3	47018.3	
65.	Tarpon	13979.5	47001.7	
66.	Quansit Hut	14011.1	46966.9	
67.	Chickasaw	14056.8	46978.6	
68.	Fountain-Bleau East	14019.8	47028.2	71' deep, 10 miles from P. City Pass
69.	PCM1 Barge	14042.8	46999.8	76' deep, 5 miles from P. City Pass
70.	Warsaw Site	14037.1	46977.5	78' deep, 6 miles from P. City Pass
71.	Midway Site	14072.4	46949.3	71' deep, 7 miles from P. City Pass

#	Reef	LOP #1	LOP #2	Notes
72.	Loss Pontoon	14078.0	46973.7	67' deep, 4 miles from P. City Pass
73.	Liberty Ship	14064.9	46918.7	75' deep, 10 miles from P. City Pass
74.	Stage 1	13979.8	46957.7	
75.	Stage 1 East	14011.3	46925.5	100' deep, 11 miles from P. City Pass
76.	Stage 2	14068.9	46997.7	

Note 1: Located 1.5 miles south of bouy "8a" which marks the center of the Pensacola Pass. The wreck is awash and marked by bell buoy "WR2."

Fishing Charters

For those who don't have a boat, there are many charter boats available that will allow you to catch fish in the Gulf under the tutelage of experienced captains. There are basically two types of fishing charter services readily available. They are **walk-on charters and private charters.**

Walk-on charters offer bottom fishing exclusively. They typically take from 10 to 50 people on a boat for half-day trips (about $25 per person) or full-day trips (about $35 per person). Your party can consist of any number from one to a boatful. In either case, make reservations in advance to secure your spot on the boat. The captains of these boats go to many of the popular bottom fishing spots as well as their private spots, which are carefully guarded trade secrets. They usually offer a nice day on the Gulf and good bottom fishing for a fair price.

Private charters are also available as half-day or full-day trips. These types of charters are more tailored to your individual desires as your party is the only group on board the vessel. They offer trolling (for everything from king mackerel to blue marlin) as well as bottom fishing and more individualized assistance when fishing. A typical price for this type of charter is $600 for up to six passengers on a full-day trip with an additional $50 per person beyond six. A typical half-day trip will run $350 for up to six passengers with an additional $45/person for those beyond six. "The Fisherman's Directory" in the back of this book lists some charter boats locally.

Chapter

4

Local Fish Recipes

The abundance and variety of local fish species have made seafood a staple along the Miracle Strip. Over the years, locals have experimented with literally thousands of different recipes for preparing freshly caught fish. This chapter provides some of the local favorite recipes.

Fried Fish Pieces

5 pounds fish fillets	1 teaspoon salt
1 1/2 cups milk	1/2 teaspoon pepper
1/2 cup Kellogg's corn flake	1 teaspoon Lawry's
crumbs	seasoned salt
1 cup flour	Peanut oil

Skin and fillet fish. Cut into bite-sized pieces. Put fish into a small bowl and cover with milk; refrigerate for 1 hour.

In a bowl, mix corn flake crumbs, flour, salt, pepper, and Lawry's salt. Roll fish in flour mixture. Fry fish in deep fryer at 400 degrees until brown, 3-5 minutes. Fry 8-10 pieces at a time, keeping oil very hot.

Yield: 10 servings

Broiled Fish

4 fish fillets (snapper, scampi, Spanish mackerel)	4 teaspoons prepared mustard
4 tablespoons butter	Parmesan cheese
4 tablespoons lemon juice	Paprika

Preheat oven to 350 degrees. Line a shallow baking dish with aluminum foil. Place fish fillets, in baking dish, skin side down. In a saucepan, melt butter. Stir in lemon juice and mustard. Pour over fish fillets. Bake for 10-20 minutes, depending on thickness of fillets. Baste several times with sauce. Sprinkle with Parmesan cheese and paprika and broil until brown and bubbly.

Yield: 4 servings

Easy and Delicious Fish

Fish fillets	Mayonnaise
Lemon juice	Parmesan cheese
Salt and pepper	Paprika

Preheat oven to 450 degrees. Wash fish and pat dry. Line a baking dish with foil. Place fish skin side down in baking dish. Squeeze lemon juice over fish; sprinkle generously with salt and pepper. Spread mayonnaise evenly over fish, including the edges. Sprinkle with Parmesan cheese and paprika. Bake for 15-20 minutes, or until done. Run under broiler for 1 minute or until lightly browned and puffed.

Yield: 1/2 pound fish per person

Grilled King Mackerel Steaks

2 pounds fresh or frozen King Mackerel steaks	2 tablespoons chopped parsley
1/4 cup orange juice	1 tablespoon lemon j
1/4 cup soy sauce	1/2 teaspoon pepper
2 tablespoons ketchup	1 clove garlic, crushed
2 tablespoons oil	1/2 teaspoon oregano

Thaw steaks if frozen. Cut into serving-size portions and place single layer in shallow baking dish. Combine remaining ingredients to make sauce and pour over fish. Let stand for 30 minutes, turning once. Remove fish, reserving sauce for basting. Place fish in well-greased hinged wire grills. Cook about 4 inches from moderately hot coals for 8 minutes. Baste with sauce. Turn and cook 7-10 minutes longer, or until fish flakes easily when tested with a fork.

Yield: 6 servings

Flounder Florentine

2 10-ounce packages frozen chopped spinach	1/2 cup half and half
2 tablespoons butter	1/2 cup fish stock
1/4 cup finely chopped onion	10 flounder fillets, skinned
2 cloves garlic, pressed	1/3 cup lemon juice
1/2 teaspoon salt	2 teaspoons Worcestershire sauce
1/4 teaspoon pepper	1/2 cup butter
1/4 teaspoon freshly grated nutmeg	2 cups finely chopped mushrooms
2 tablespoons butter	2 tablespoons flour
2 tablespoons flour	1 cup sour cream
	1/2 cup Parmesan cheese

Cook spinach according to package directions. Drain well. Set aside. In a heavy skillet, melt 2 tablespoons butter and saute onion and garlic. Add drained spinach, salt, pepper, and nutmeg. Simmer 4 minutes.

In a heavy saucepan, melt 2 tablespoons butter over medium-high heat. Add flour; cook, stirring constantly, until mixture is bubbling. Add half and half and fish stock. Continue stirring until sauce is thick and smooth. Add white sauce to spinach mixture and stir well. Remove from heat.

Preheat oven to 400 degrees. Place a spoonful of spinach mixture on each flounder fillet. Roll up and place seam-side down in a buttered baking dish. In a small saucepan, melt 1/2 cup butter. Add Worcestershire sauce and lemon juice; pour over fillets. Cover baking dish with foil and bake for 20 minutes.

Pour liquid from fish into a skillet and saute mushrooms until most of the liquid is reduced. Remove from heat. Combine flour and sour cream; gently stir into mushrooms. Pour over fish and sprinkle with cheese. Brown fish lightly under broiler.

Yield: 8 servings

Redfish

2 to 3 pounds redfish	1 tablespoon dry white
Salt and pepper	wine
1 pound butter	Parmesan cheese
Lemon juice	paprika

Preheat oven to 400 degrees. Fillet fish and sprinkle with salt and pepper. Put butter into shallow baking pan in hot oven until it is browned. Place fillets flesh-side down in sizzling hot butter and return pan to oven for 10 - 15 minutes. Turn fillets with spatula and baste with pan juices. Sprinkle each piece with lemon juice, wine, cheese and paprika. Return to oven until done, about 5 minutes. Then broil for 1 minute. Baste fish with sauce.

Yield: 4 servings (This recipe works well for any fish fillet.)

Polynesian Fish Dish

3 pounds snapper, scamp, or any similar fish, cut into fillets	1/2 teaspoon marjoram
	1/2 can cream of shrimp soup
1/3 cup lime juice	1/2 cup sour cream
1/4 cup butter, melted	3 green onions and tops, thinly sliced
1/2 teaspoon salt	
1/4 teaspoon pepper	1/2 cup tiny boiled shrimp

Wash fish and pat dry. Place in shallow oven-proof baking dish. Pour lime juice over fish and marinate 15 minutes. Pour off lime juice and pour melted butter over fish. Sprinkle with salt, pepper, and marjoram. Broil 10 minutes; baste with pan juices. Cool slightly. Mix soup and sour cream; spoon some over each piece of fish. Garnish with onion and shrimp. Bake in a preheated 350-degree oven until thoroughly heated.

Yield: 6 servings

Red Snapper with Sour Cream Dressing

1/2 cup chopped onion	3 pounds red snapper fillets
1 cup chopped celery	
1/2 cup butter, melted	Lemon juice

1/2 cup dry bread crumbs	Salt
1/2 cup sour cream	Paprika
1/4 cup lemon, peeled and diced	Chopped parsley

Preheat oven to 350 degrees. Combine onion, celery, butter, bread crumbs, sour cream, and lemon. Spread mixture in a greased baking dish. Place fillets on top and season with lemon juice, salt, paprika, and parsley. Bake for 30-40 minutes, depending on thickness of fillets. Fish is done when it flakes, but is not dry.

Yield: 6 servings

Red Snapper Veracruz Style

3 pounds fresh snapper fillets	Flour
2 tablespoons fresh lime juice	Salt and pepper
1 teaspoon salt	Vegetable oil for frying
	3 tablespoons olive oil

Sprinkle fish with lime juice and salt; set aside for two hours. While fish marinates, prepare sauce.

Sauce:

1/4 cup olive oil	1 large bay leaf
1 medium onion, thinly sliced	1/4 teaspoon oregano
2 large cloves garlic, peeled and sliced	12 pitted green olives, halved
2 pounds fresh tomatoes, peeled, seeded, and chopped	2 tablespoons capers
	2 pickled jalapenos, cut into strips
	Salt

Heat oil and cook onion and garlic until tender but not brown. Add remaining ingredients and simmer about 30 minutes.

Preheat oven to 325 degrees. Dredge fish in flour, seasoned with salt and pepper, and fry in hot oil until golden brown. Place in a large baking dish or in individual baking dishes and top with sauce. Sprinkle top of sauce with olive oil and bake uncovered about 20 minutes or until just tender.

This can also be done with a whole 3-pound snapper. Cook 30 minutes.

Yield: 6 - 8 servings

Trout Amandine

1 1/2 cup half and half	Flour
3 eggs	Vegetable oil for frying
1 teaspoon salt	2 cups sliced almonds
1/2 teaspoon white pepper	1 cup butter
3 pounds fresh speckled trout, filleted and skinned	Lemon wedges

Make a batter of half and half, eggs, salt, and white pepper. Dredge fish in flour; dip into batter and then into flour again. Fry in hot oil until golden brown. Drain on paper towels. Saute' almonds in butter until golden brown. Serve fish topped with almonds and garnished with a wedge of lemon.

Yield: 6 servings

These recipes as well as many others (from soups to desserts) are published in The Junior League of Pensacola's cookbook, *SOME LIKE IT SOUTH!* Proceeds from the sale of *SOME LIKE IT SOUTH!* are returned to the community through the programs and projects of The Junior League of Pensacola, Inc.

Appendix A:
Fish Identification Charts

This appendix will help you identify what you catch. While comprehensive coverage of the many fish in the Gulf is beyond the scope of this book, some of the most popular and common fish are included here.

* Sketches courtesy of Great Outdoors Publishing.

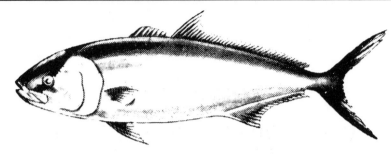

* Amberjack

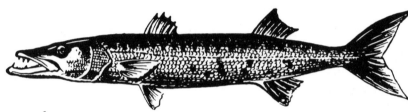

* Barracuda

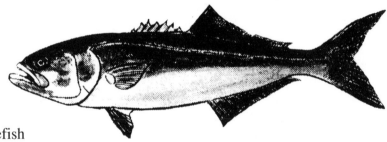

* Bluefish

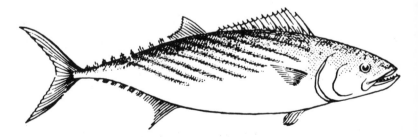

* Bonito

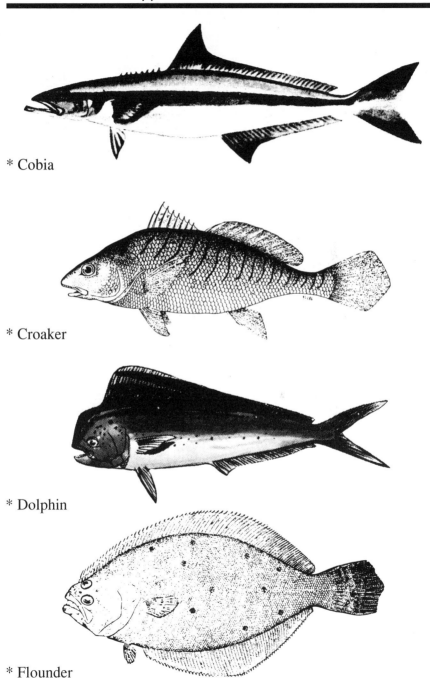

* Cobia

* Croaker

* Dolphin

* Flounder

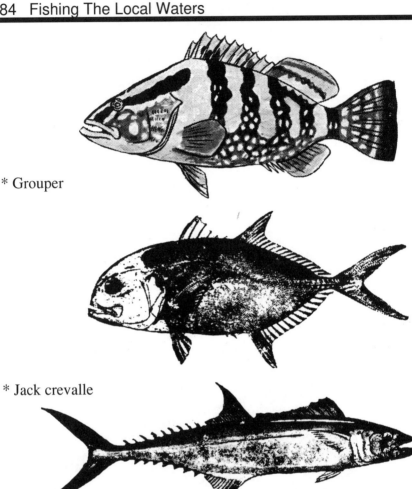

* Grouper

* Jack crevalle

* King mackerel

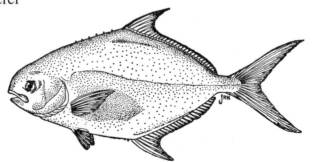

* Pompano

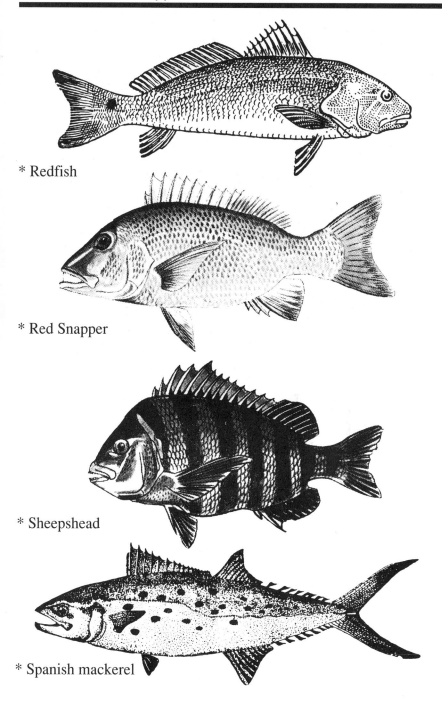

* Redfish

* Red Snapper

* Sheepshead

* Spanish mackerel

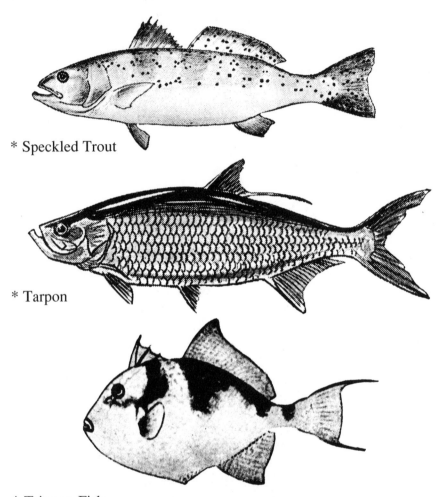

* Speckled Trout

* Tarpon

* Trigger Fish

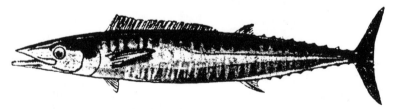

* Wahoo

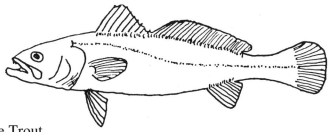

* White Trout

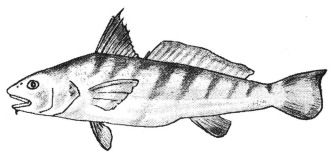

* Whiting

Appendix B:
Area Maps

This appendix will help you find the fishing spots described in Chapters 1 and 2. There are four maps included:

* Gulf Shores
* Pensacola
* Ft. Walton/Destin
* Panama City

The fishing spots discussed in Chapters 1 and 2 are marked on these maps.

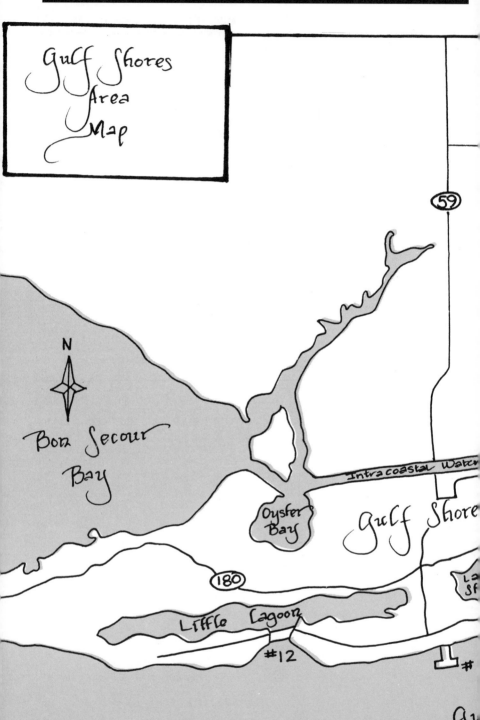

Gulf Shores
Area
Map

N

Bon Secour
Bay

Oyster
Bay

Gulf Shore

Intracoastal Water

59

180

Little Lagoon

#12

La
SF

Elberta

98   98

Foley

83

29

Wolf Bay

Perdido Bay

#1   180

161

2

180

Ono Island

#2   Perdido Key

of Mexico

#1 Intracoastal Canal
#2 Alabama Point
#12 West Pass
#13 Alabama State
       Fishing Pier

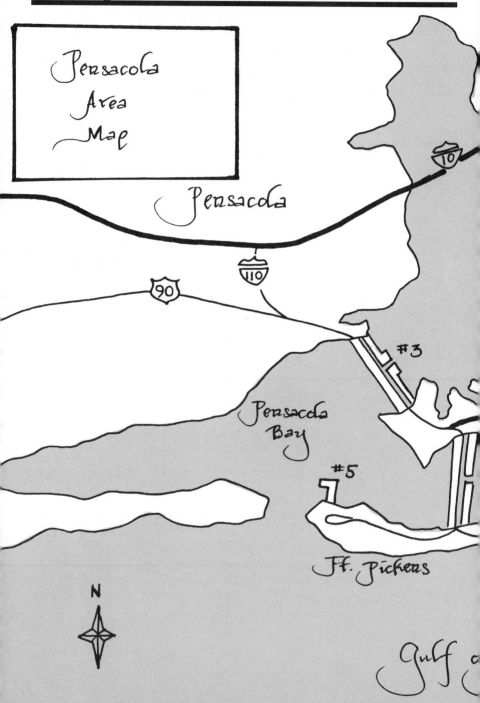

Escambia Bay

87

98

Gulf Breeze

Santa Rosa Sound

#6

399

Pensacola Beach

#15

Navarre
Beach

#14

Mexico

#3 Old Bay Bridge
#4 Old Beach Bridge
#5 Ft. Pickens Pier
#6 Navarre Bridge
#14 Pensacola Beach
       Fishing Pier
#15 Navarre Beach
       Fishing Pier

Ft. Walton
   Destin
Area
      Map

Ft. Walton
Beach

N

Cinco
Bayou

#8

Mary Esther

Santa Rosa
Sound

#98

Ft. Walton
Beach

#7 East Pass Channel Bridge
#8 Cinco Bayou Bridge
#9 garnier Bayou Bridge
#16 Okaloosa island Pier
#17 East Pass Jetty

gulf

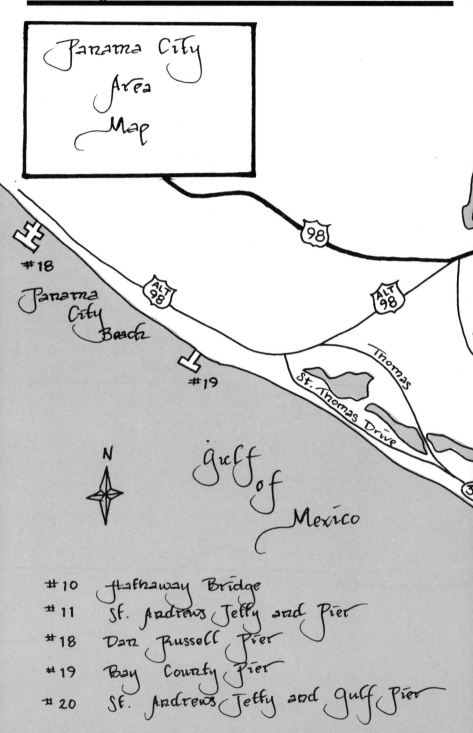

Panama City
Area
Map

#18

Panama City Beach

#19

98

ALT 98

ALT 98

St. Thomas Drive

Thomas

3

N

Gulf of Mexico

#10   Hathaway Bridge
#11   St. Andrews Jetty and Pier
#18   Dan Russell Pier
#19   Bay County Pier
#20   St. Andrews Jetty and Gulf Pier

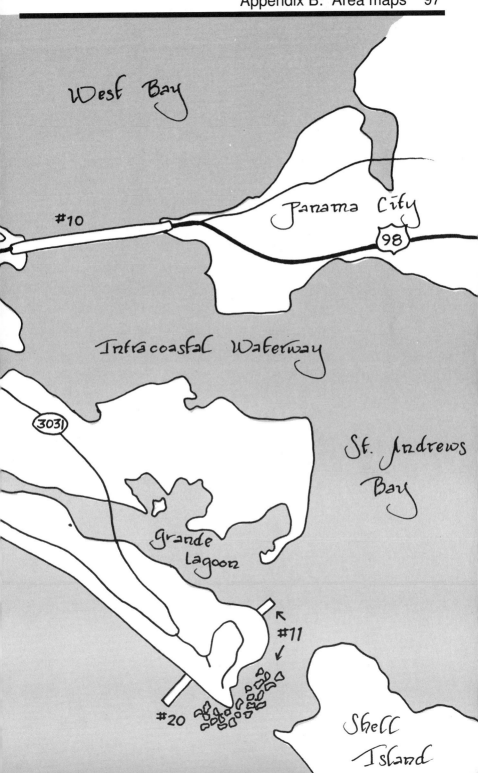

The Fisherman's Directory

A Guide to local businesses that cater to fishermen

Gulf Shores Area

Bait/tackle shops

Childre, Lew Pro Shop 943-1467
Curiosity Shop 492-2516

E-Z Tackle Shop 943-5729
Frith's Bait & Supply 968-6484
Gulf State Park Fishing Pier 948-7275
J & M Tackle 981-5460

Orange Beach Hardware 981-6323
Orange Beach Marina 981-4207
Outrigger 981-4251

Perdido Pass Marina 981-6481
Sams Stop-n-Shop 981-4245
Zeke's Landing 981-4007

To place an ad in the next edition, contact:

Maximum Press
605 Silverthorn Road
Gulf Breeze, FL 32561
(904) 934-0819

Pensacola Area

Bait/Tackle Shops

Ace Hardware	932-3687
Bob's Ship Store	934-1005
Dolphin Marine	438-6637
Gray's Tackle Shop	934-3151
Gray's Bait and Tackle II	492-2666
Gulf Breeze Bait & Tackle	932-6789
Hanco #255	492-3800
Innerarity Hardware	492-1149
Letts Lures	476-4384
McCrory's	932-3318
Major League Sport.Goods	968-6087

Pensacola Area
(Continued)

Navarre Beach Fishing Pier	939-3869	Sherman Cove (Navy base)	452-3369
NAS Exchange (Navy Base)	456-5701	Smiths Bait & Tackle	944-6396
One Stop Bait and Tackle	433-2962	Southern Sportsman	479-4500
Outcast Bait & Tackle	492-1839	Sunny Beach	455-4541
		Swamp House Landing	478-9906
Penny's Sporting Goods	438-9633		
Pens. Beach Fishing Pier	932-0444	Walts Bait & Tackle	478-9585
Phils Bait & Tackle	476-6844	Wright Tackle Shop Inc	432-4558
Rod Arts 456-0047			
Ross Stores	492-0424		
Sandpiper Distributing	492-0497		

August 7th & 8th, 1993
Gulf Breeze, Florida

Ft. Walton/Destin Area

Bait/Tackle Shops

4 Season Bait & Tackle 836-4860
Alaqua Bait & Oyster Bar ... 835-9890
Anns Bait Shop 835-9891
Aquatic Enterprises Inc 243-5721

Baker Marine 243-8384
Bay Town Marina 267-7777
Club Nautico Marina 937-6811

Destin Blue chip 837-3910
Destin Fishin Hole 837-9043

Destin Fighing Hole II 243-7191
Destin Ice house 837-8333
East Pass Marina 837-2622
Galley Marine 654-1635
Half Hitch II 837-3212
Okaloosa Island Pier 244-1023

Paradise 98 Sports 837-5941
Pats Market 244-9934

Quality Reel Repair 862-0885
Quick Way Foods Store 729-1121
Reds Place 837-7853

Ft. Walton/Destin Area
(Continued)

Salty Bass 863-7999
Stewarts Outdoor Sports 243-9443
The Ships Chandler 837-9306
Vaughns Gun & Tackle 682-8244

Panama City Area
Bait/Tackle Shops

Bayside Marina 234-6668
Bell Tackle Co. 763-0241
Brooks Groc. Bait & Tackle 871-2863
C and G Sporting Goods 769-2317
Cedar Creek Bait Ranch 265-9587

D J's Groc. & Beach Supp. .. 234-3941
Dan Russel Pier (Halfhitch) . 233-5080
Deerpoint Bait & Tackle 763-1494
Forest Park Bait & Tackle ... 763-5646

Half Hitch Tackle 234-2621
Hancocks Cut Off 785-5416

Holiday Lodge Marina 235-2809
Howell Tackle Supply Inc .. 785-8548
Libbys Fishing Supplies 265-9057
Panama City Marina Svcs ... 785-0161
Panama City Bch Pier
    Tackle Shop 235-2576
Panhandle Ice Co 785-8677
Pilcher Bait & Tackle Shop 785-6518
Port Panama City Marina 785-0551

St. Andrews State Park 233-5140
Sun Harbour Marina 785-0551
Treasure Island 234-6533

Index